BIG BAD
BIBLE GIANTS

BIG BAD
BIBLE GIANTS

WRITTEN BY
ED**STRAUSS**

ILLUSTRATED BY
ANTHONY**CARPENTER**

Zonder**kidz**

Zonder**kidz**®

The children's group of Zondervan
www.zonderkidz.com

Big Bad Bible Giants
Copyright © 2005 by Ed Strauss
Illustrations Copyright © 2005 by The Zondervan Corporation

Requests for information should be addressed to:
Grand Rapids, Michigan 49530

ISBN: 0-310-70869-9

Library of Congress Cataloging-in-Publication Data

Strauss, Ed, 1953-
  Big bad Bible giants / by Ed Strauss.
      p. cm.
  ISBN 0-310-70869-9 (softcover)
  1. Giants in the Bible--Juvenile literature. I. Title.

  BS1199.G5A77 2004
  220.9'5--dc22
                                                                        2004011826

Editor: Amy De Vries
Interior design: Merit Alderink
Art direction: Merit Alderink & Michelle Lenger

Printed in United States of America

05 06 07 / RRD / 5 4 3 2 1

CONTENTS

WHAT'S THIS BOOK ABOUT ANYWAY?

You might've thought this book would be all about Goliath. You know, the big guy who attacked David and got a rock in the head for his trouble. Goliath was just one of many giants who were holed up in Gath. There were gobs of others.

Even these gigantic goons weren't the greatest and most powerful of all giants. No way! At one time, thousands of giants ruled the mountains and valleys of Canaan (see map on page 10). Goliath and his gang were just the last of this nearly extinct race. (Not stinky. Extinct. Well, okay, they probably were stinky too.)

In this book, you'll find out where these fearsome foul-tempered monsters came from, how they lived, how much food they devoured, and how they fought battles. We'll give you the lowdown on how huge they were—nine to eleven feet tall—and why they died out. (It wasn't all from rocks in the head.)

Bonus: you'll also learn about the incredibly gutsy, godly guys who fought and conquered them!

Modern Giants ... Almost

You're probably thinking that we just named the tallest dudes on earth, 'cause the tallest guys all play basketball. Right? Wrong. Some of them do, but not all. Really tall, skinny guys get more easily injured on the court, so some of the tallest guys keep out of basketball. Let's look at some of the tallest people in modern history.

- Robert P. Wadlow—Height: 8'11" Weight: 490 lb. According to *The Guinness Book of World Records*, he was the world's tallest man on record. Wadlow was an American from Alton, Illinois. He was born in 1918, and by the time he was eight, he was 6 feet tall and weighed 170 pounds. By the time he was thirteen, Rob was 7 feet 4 inches tall and weighed about 280 pounds. When he died in 1940, at twenty-two years of age, he was 8 feet 11 inches and weighed 490 pounds! (He wore a foot brace to support his weight, and it caused an infection that killed him.)

- Patrick Cotter O'Brien (1761–1806)—Height: 8' 3.5". This Irishman often went on exhibition tours to earn money (meaning he earned a living by letting people stare at him).

- Don Koehler (1925–1981)—Height: 8' 2". Born in Denton, Montana, Don was a normal-sized kid until he was ten years old. Then he began shooting up, up, up till he was 8 feet 2 inches tall.

- Mohammad Alam Channa (1956–1998)—Height: 7' 7". At 7 feet 7 inches tall, this guy from Pakistan held the title of the world's tallest man for some years.

- Naseer Ahmaad Soomro—Height: 7' 8.9". Naseer, from Pakistan, was the tallest man on earth for a while. He lost his title in 1999.

- Radhouane Charbib—Height: 7' 8.9". Rad is from Tunisia in northern Africa, and at 7 feet 8.9 inches, he soon held the title of the tallest man on earth!

- Hussain Bisad—Height: 7' 9". Hussain is from Somalia and he's 7 feet 9 inches tall. Do the math. Hussain is one-tenth of an inch taller than Rad Charbib.

- Michael and James Lanier—Height: 7' 6". These two Americans are 7 feet 6 inches tall and also hold a world record. How? They're the tallest twins on the planet. They both played collegiate basketball.

- Zeng Jinlian—Height: 8' 1.75". The tallest woman in modern history was Zeng Jinlian from China. She was 8 feet 1.75 inches tall.

- Sandy Allen—Height: 7' 7.25". She is the tallest woman alive in the United States.

Are any of these guys or gals giants? No. Only Robert Wadlow came even close. But even Rob was still nearly a foot shorter than Goliath.

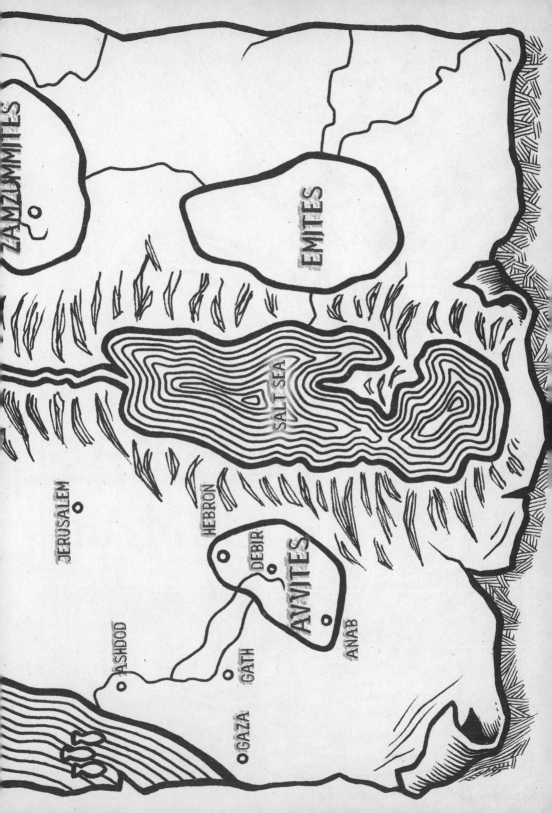

TALL TALES AND BRITISH GIANTS

You may be thinking, "What? Nine to eleven feet tall? That's no giant! A giant is 200 feet tall, like Paul Bunyan—a guy so big, he single-handedly chopped down all the trees in North and South Dakota, carved out the Great Lakes with his ax, and ... and ... had a dinosaur-sized blue ox following him around, too, I bet. Now that's a giant!"

Actual giants were big, but they weren't that big! But before we get to giants from the Bible, let's look at giants in tales and legends.

Some of the most famous fairy-tale giants are from England, like the ones in the story Jack the Giant-Killer. Jack lived in the days of King Arthur, when a giant named Cormoran was supposedly ter-rorizing southwest England. Jack dug a pit and Cormoran— not particularly bright—tumbled into it. Jack outsmarted several more dim-witted giants in the land of Wales.

Gods in Myths

A myth is an imaginary story, and Greek myths talk about a race of giants named Titans who attacked the biggest Greek god-guy, Zeus. As punishment, the Titans were dropped into the lowest basement of hell. The Vikings had the same kind of myths: They believed that a colossal race of giants tried to attack the Viking gods.

So what's with these stories? We know that the Greek and Viking gods were made up, but is there any truth to giant humans? Well, we don't know whether giants ever roamed the green hills of Wales, and if they fought imaginary gods, well, duh, that would be a waste of their time, wouldn't it?

Wales has so many legends about giants that everywhere you turn, people point out, "Oh yeah, a giant used to live there" or "See that mountain? There's a giant buried on top of it."

Maybe giants once lived there, maybe they didn't. But two things we know for sure are: (1) nations all around the world have legends about giants, and (2) thousands of years ago, giants definitely roamed this planet. The Bible says, "There were giants in the earth in those days" (Genesis 6:4 KJV).

SURLY AND SNARLY

Another thing most legends say is that giants weren't just huge and strong but also mean, foul-tempered, and surly. Giants seemed to always be ticked off. They always got up on the wrong side of the bed. And they never combed their hair or bathed or used mouthwash.

Legend says that when giants got hungry, they'd simply step over your fence, grab your milk cow, and carry it off. They had massive clubs to bash people with, and—so the stories go—some giants even ate humans! They were the sort of neighbors you'd rather not have.

A famous Christian writer named John Bunyan—not related to the big lumberjack—wrote about people-eating giants in

Pilgrim's Progress. His book was an allegory, which teaches spiritual truths. He talked about the bones of pilgrims scattered in front of a cave where two giants lived. (In the story, pilgrims represent Christians on their spiritual journey, and giants represent dangers in a Christian's path.) Yup. Not only were these giants cannibals, but they were also messy. Imagine these guys living in your bedroom! Pigsty? Oh yeah!

In Bunyan's book, a giant named Giant Despair chucked two pilgrims, Christian and Hopeful, into his castle dungeon and beat them black and blue with a crab-tree club. Then a knight named Sir Great-heart killed another giant, named Giant Maul, plus a people-eating giant called Slay-good.

The Bible never says that giants ate people, but when David fought Goliath, Goliath told him, "I'll give your flesh to the birds of the air and the beasts of the field!" (1 Samuel 17:44). That's not quite like the giant in Jack and the Beanstalk saying, "Be he alive or be he dead, I'll grind his bones to make my bread!" But it works out the same: David would be killed by a giant, then gobbled up.

Gigantic Facts

Okay, let's pause here and ask a basic question: could humans really grow to giant sizes? Well, why not? We know there used to be giant animals. Check these out:

- Nowadays, pigs are usually only three feet tall, and a really big porker only weighs 500 pounds. Thousands of years ago, relatives of modern pigs called entelodonts were six and a half feet tall and weighed 2,000 pounds—one ton! That's a lot of pork.

- Sloths today only grow a couple feet long and are so light, they hang up in branches. Way back when, ground sloths named *Megatherium* were twenty feet tall on their hind legs and weighed as much as an elephant!

- Ostriches are the biggest flightless birds today. They grow eight feet tall and weigh 345 pounds. Impressive? Huh! A few hundred years ago, 1,000-pound elephant birds stomped around Madagascar, and fifteen-foot-tall moas crashed through the forests of New Zealand.

- Today gorillas are six feet tall when standing upright and weigh 400 pounds. Thousands of years ago in China, gorillas named *Gigantopithecus* stood ten feet tall and weighed—get this—1,200 pounds!

- And what about people? Today the average man is about five feet nine inches tall and weighs 150 pounds. A few thousand years ago, a race of humans called Rephaites grew nine and a half to eleven feet tall and weighed 850 to 1,200 pounds. You guessed it. They were giants!

GIANTS' TREASURE

In legends, giants gathered treasure by robbing travelers. Bottom line: any hero brave enough to battle them could grab their treasure. In Jack and the Beanstalk, Jack ran off with a golden harp and a goose that laid golden eggs. The giant who lived at the top of the beanstalk tried to follow, but Jack chopped down the huge plant and—ker-whummp!— Mr. Giant skydived to earth. Without a parachute.

A goose that laid golden eggs? Whoa! That's wild! But did giants actually have treasure? Yup. Some did. Nearly 4,000 years ago in Canaan, they lived in fortresses and ruled over the surrounding villages. According to Canaanite customs, they demanded tribute from normal-sized villagers. Tribute is "protection money"—meaning, "You pay me money and I'll protect you from enemy invaders."

Real giants probably were foul-tempered, and it had to do with their size. You see, being ten feet tall and weighing 900 pounds always got a guy to the front of the food line, but it had its drawbacks. Giants were so heavy, they tired out quickly. Result? They didn't run around much and were usually slow and lazy. And being so huge made them clumsy, meaning they had more accidents. Plus their bones probably ached from all that weight. And they probably had heart and lung disease. But hey! Learn a giant lesson: Feeling bad is no excuse to always go around in a surly, snarly mood, like a nightmare neighbor. Don't take your problems out on other people.

THE FALLEN ONES

Giants appeared on earth sometime before Noah's flood. Genesis 6:4 says, "The Nephilim were on the earth in those days—and also afterward—when the sons of God went to the daughters of men and had children by them. They were the heroes of old, men of renown."

The word *Nephilim* means "Fallen Ones," but some translations use the word *giants* instead. This is because the Bible says the Nephilim were giant-sized and strong. The spies who scouted out Canaan told Moses, "All the people we saw there are of great size. We saw the Nephilim there" (Numbers 13:32–33).

Ten-Foot Tall Sons

Who were these sons of God marrying the daughters of men? Some Bible scholars say they were the sons of godly Seth marrying the daughters of evil Cain (Genesis 4:8, 25–26). Maybe so, but when normal-sized people marry normal-sized people, it doesn't usually produce ten-foot-tall kids with muscles like the Incredible Hulk's.

Other scholars say that "sons of God" means "angels," because angels are called "sons of God" in other places in the Bible. In Job 1:6, the original Hebrew says that the "sons of God" came before God. The New International Version translates those words as "angels."

Angels are a different kind of being, so they're obviously not supposed to marry humans. Any angels that did that would have to be evil and disobedient. If that's actually where giants came from, then—whooeeee—no wonder giants were famous for being bad!

The Heroes of Old

Josephus, a Jewish scholar who lived in Jesus' day, said that the evil acts of the Nephilim reminded him of the Titans, the giants in the Greek myths who rebelled against Zeus. Some Christians think that when the Greeks made up their stories about giants, they were copying the true stories about giants in the Bible. That may be what happened. We don't know.

What Giants Looked Like

Giants were huge and fearsome, but what did they look like? In fairy tales they're usually ugly and have brutish scowls, deep-set eyes, huge noses, and messy black beards. They're also very hairy and look like they desperately need a bath.

That may not be far from the truth. The Bible doesn't tell us what the Rephaites looked like, but Josephus described them. He said, "The race of giants ... had bodies so large, and countenances [faces] so entirely different from other men, that they were surprising to the sight, and terrible to the hearing."

Wow! Faces "entirely different from other men" must have been shocking! And if Josephus was right about giants being "terrible to the hearing," they probably had deep voices and shouted like human foghorns. Imagine trying to get to sleep at night if your giant neighbors were arguing!

Now, some people think all giants had six fingers on each hand and six toes on each foot, just because one giant in the Bible did (2 Samuel 21:20). Not likely. The Bible makes a big deal out of saying that giant had twenty-four fingers and toes, which shows he was an exception.

HIGH WATERS

First the Bible says that giant Nephilim were stomping around the earth before the Flood, and then it says, "The LORD saw how great man's wickedness on the earth had become" (Genesis 6:5). Sounds like the Nephilim were especially wicked. Jewish people have many legends about how horrible and gross the giants were.

The Bible calls Noah "a preacher of righteousness" (2 Peter 2:5). Josephus said that Noah went to the giants and urged them to change their evil ways, but they didn't listen. Noah was afraid the giants would kill him, so he grabbed his wife and kids and ran. Did this really happen? We don't know. One thing we do know is that only eight people from the old earth survived: Noah and his wife, his three sons, and their wives. That was it. No other humans survived the Flood—and that means no giants survived, either. They were gone, buried under millions of tons of water and mud (Genesis 7:13, 23–24).

GET SMARTER

Many Christians believe that the "sons of God" who married "the daughters of men" were evil angels and that their children were Frankenstein-type beings called giants. They say that 2 Peter 2:4 talks about these angels: "God did not spare angels when they sinned, but sent them to hell, putting them into gloomy dungeons." These are good guesses and might be true, but it's important to remember that they're only guesses. The Bible doesn't give a lot of details about how giants originated. We don't know for sure if the "sons of God" were angels or that God later slammed them into prison. The angel-and-giant theory might be right, but it might be wrong. It's fine to wonder about mysterious things like "Where did giants come from?" but always remember the difference between facts and theories.

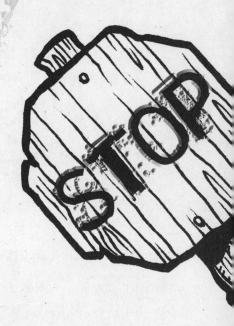

Giants After the Flood

"Wait a second," you say. "Giants lived on the earth after the Flood, too! If all the Nephilim were wiped out in the Flood, where did Goliath and all these other giants come from afterward?" Good question. Here are a couple possibilities.

- *Giants lived in the land of Canaan, and Canaan was Ham's son, so maybe Ham's wife had some giant ancestors. Then a few of their descendants grew giant-sized, and next thing you know— giants on the earth again.*

- *Maybe the large people the Hebrew spies saw weren't Nephilim (Numbers 13:17–33). The spies might've been exaggerating. After all, they were trying to scare the Israelites.*

Bottom line? You may hear others say they know all about where giants came from, before and after the Flood, but nobody knows for certain.

Tall as Trees

Noah had a son called Ham, Ham had a son called Bacon ... Just joking. Okay, seriously, Ham had a son named Canaan, and

Canaan had some descendants called Amorites. In Joshua's day Amorites lived all over Canaan (Genesis 10:1, 6, 15–16; Numbers 13:29).

God told the Israelites, "I destroyed the Amorite before [you], though he was tall as the cedars and strong as the oaks... I brought you up out of Egypt ... to give you the land of the Amorites" (Amos 2:9–10). Now, most Amorites were just regular-sized people, but if—and this is a big if—some of them were actually "tall as the cedars and strong as the oaks," that sounds like some of the Amorites were giants!

PAPA GIANT

When the Bible refers to "The Giant," it calls him "Rapha" (2 Samuel 21:16, 18), and when it talks about many giants—his descendants—it calls them Rephaites.

We don't know much about Rapha. What we do know about him is that the Rephaites were descended from him and were named after him. We also know they lived for over two thousand years in Canaan with the Canaanites and Amorites.

GRANDDADDY OF GIANT-KILLERS

Most of the giant-killers in the Bible were Israelites, and Abraham (Abram) was the father of the Israelites. About 4,000 years ago, he came into Canaan with his herders driving his flocks and herds. Abraham's wife, Sarah, was with him, and Abe's nephew Lot tagged along. The Canaanites and Amorites already lived there. Giants lived there, too—lots of them (Numbers 13:29; Deuteronomy 2:10, 21).

In fact, by the time Abraham entered Canaan, the Rephaites had separated into six different clans: the Emites, the Zamzummites, the Rephaites of Bashan, the Rephaites of North Canaan, the Avvites, and the Anakites of Hebron.

So here comes this pint-size shepherd. Abraham was seventy-five years old, normal height, and average weight. Compare that with thousands of giant-sized, heavyweight Rephaites!

Now think of Abraham's faith! When God told Abraham he'd give the land of the Rephaites to his descendants, Abraham believed (Genesis 12:4; 15:18–20). Abraham was normal-sized but his faith was giganto-normous!

GIANTS' HERO

The giants may have seemed invincible but they weren't. Kedorlaomer, the king of Elam, gathered his armies and four other kings' armies and attacked the land east of the Jordan River, where the Emites, Zamzummites, and Rephaites of Bashan lived (Genesis 14:5). And Kedorlaomer and all his armies defeated the giants! Wow! They must've had a huge army!

Think that was impressive? Get this! Kedorlaomer and his armies were strutting along, boasting about defeating the giants, when little old Abraham whistled for his shepherds, called his Amorite allies, then pounded these five kings' armies (Genesis 14:14–16). Tough? You got that right!

raham defeated the guys who defeated the giants! (But really, he
dn't been out to avenge the giants. He was just trying to rescue his
phew Lot.)

GET COOLER

Giants lived for 2,000 years among normal-sized
Canaanites. Does that mean they were peace-loving,
good neighbors? Not necessarily. They were probably
pretty oppressive and had the little Canaanites slav-
ing away, doing their work for them. Plus they'd have
made nearby little-guy villagers pay protection money.
In other words, they were bullies. You probably know
kids like that at your school. But as Abraham found
out, these grizzly-bear-sized bozos were not invincible. In fact, because Abraham had the courage to
do the right thing and God was on his side, soon the
Rephaites were looking up to him. It may not always
work out that way for you, but take a tip: it pays to
trust God and do the right thing.

Journey to the Emites

Let's zero in on the six giant clans who lived in Canaan. Look at the map (pages 10-11) and you'll see that east of the Dead Sea is high plateau land called Moab. Grapes grow well there, and the high country has good grazing for cattle and sheep (Numbers 32:1; 2 Kings 3:4).

There weren't any Moabites back in Abraham's day. These high pasture hills were ruled by a clan of giants called Emites. Deuteronomy 2:10–11 says, "The Emites used to live there—a people strong and numerous, and as tall as the Anakites. Like the Anakites, they too were considered Rephaites, but the Moabites called them Emites." (Although other giant clans—the Avvites and the Rephaites—did have their own names, the Hebrews lumped them all together. To them all giants in Canaan were simply Anakites. Well, giants are giants, whatever name they go by.)

Besides being big and strong and tall, the Emites were numerous—meaning there were oodles of them. (Yeah, you could say these giants had giant families.) The Emites and their kids were probably cattle herders and shepherds. And good ones! Desert raiders probably thought twice before swooping down on their flocks!

Basketball Players

Basketball players are some of the tallest guys going. Most of them are between six and seven feet tall. Of course, there are really tall players like Manute Bol and Yao Ming, the Chinese basketball superstar. Let's look at some famous basketball heights and weights.

- Michael Jordan is six feet six inches and weighs 216 pounds.

- Magic Johnson is six feet nine inches and weighs 255 pounds.

- Shaq O'Neal is seven feet one inch and weighs 350 pounds.

- Seo Jang-hoon of Korea is seven feet five inches and weighs 308 pounds.

- Yao Ming from China is seven feet five inches and weighs 293 pounds.

- Manute Bol from Sudan is seven feet seven inches adn weighs 240 pounds.

But compare these guys with Goliath of Gath, who was nine feet nine inches tall and weighed about 850 pounds. That's nearly four feet taller than a full-grown male gorilla standing up, and over twice as heavy as a gorilla! Ho! How would you like to have stepped in his path to block him when he thundered down the court? Goliath would've stomped the competition. Literally. Problem was, they didn't have basketball in Goliath's day (it wasn't invented till 1891), so he joined the army.

Then one day the Moabites took over the Emites' land. The Moabites were descendants of Moab, Lot's son. The Bible doesn't say the Moabites beat the Emites in battle. It just says God gave them the Emites' land (Genesis 14:9; 19:36–37; Deuteronomy 2:9).

We don't know how many Emites were left when the Moabites showed up, but there were some, because the

Moabites knew about them and called them Emites, which means "The Terrible Ones." That gives you an idea of how they behaved. The last surviving giants probably attacked the Moabites or ran off with their sheep. Big sisters probably told their little Moabite brothers, "You behave or the Emites are gonna get you!"

ZOOM TO THE ZAMZUMMITES

The land of Ammon was rich grazing land north of Moab and south of the Jabbok River, but back in Abraham's day, this country belonged to the Zuzim, otherwise known as the

Zamzummites. (Betcha can't say "Zamzummites" ten times really fast.)

The Zamzummites were probably cattle herders and shepherds, too, but these boys weren't as laid back as the Emites' clan. Zamzummites means "Powerful, Vigorous." Now, vigorous describes someone who has a lot of power and who is active and uses that power. It also means they probably sweat a lot—and this was in the days before deodorant.

Like the Emites, the Zamzummites were conquered by King Kedorlaomer. But unlike the Emites, the Zamzummites bounced back. They were either tougher or their cities were more fortified or maybe both.

The Zamzummites were so numerous that their country was called a land of giants: "That too was considered a land of the Rephaites, who used to live there; but the Ammonites called them Zamzummites. They were a people strong and numerous, and as tall as the Anakites" (Deuteronomy 2:20–21). Imagine a land full of thousands of energetic, sweaty giants!

But all their strength and energy didn't save them when Ammon's kids showed up. Ammon's descendants were the first giant-killers mentioned in the Bible. They were just normal-sized guys, and the Zamzummites were ten to eleven feet tall and had walled cities. But the Ammonites conquered them!

How? Simple. God was with the Ammonites!

GET COOLER

In Deuteronomy 2:19 God said, "I have given [the land of the Zamzummites] as a possession to the descendants of Lot." Verse 21 adds, "The LORD destroyed [the Zamzummites] from before the Ammonites, who drove them out and settled in their place." Wow! The children of Lot could do a lot when God fought for them. God himself gave the Ammonites the land! Of course, the Ammonites still had to do their part and fight to drive the giants out, but God helped them big-time!

What about you? Have a goal that's too big for you to reach all by yourself? Hey, God's on your side, so do your part, put your plans in God's hands, and pray for his help. God will help you make your dreams come true. He's bigger than any obstacles.

SWIM TO BASHAN'S REPHAITES

If you wandered farther north in Canaan, you'd cross the Jabbok River and come to the Yarmuk River (see the map on pages 10-11). (Wading across rivers, by the way, was easy for giants.) Congrats! You are now in Bashan, the land of the Rephaites. These giants lived in the most fertile part of Bashan. Great forests of oak trees grew there—and lush green grass, so Bashan was famous for its herds of fat cattle (Psalm 22:12; Isaiah 2:13).

The giants of Bashan were very prosperous—and probably fat. Now, if an overgrown giant like Og, the king of these giants, weighed 1,200-some pounds—the top of the normal weight range for giants—how much would a fat giant have weighed? Some probably got over 1,400 pounds.

How Did They Get So Big?

When someone grows really big, they suffer from a condition called gigantism. You're probably wondering, "What causes them to grow so big?" Well, the same thing that causes all people to grow—only lots more of it!

Growth is caused by several things, but mostly by a small gland in your body called the pituitary (pih-TOO-ih-terry) gland. It's about the size of a pea and hangs out under your brain, in the center of your skull. (If you shake your head from side to side, you can hear it rattling. Okaaay. Just kidding.)

The front half of your pituitary gland produces a chemical called growth hormone. As you might have guessed, this is what makes you grow. From the moment you're born, it causes your body to create more and more cells so you grow heavier and taller. Giants' pituitary glands were very busy little peas indeed and pumped megadoses of grow-juice into their bodies.

For hundreds of years, the Rephaites of Bashan had lived in fortified cities. Just the same, Kedorlaomer's armies conquered their capital, Ashteroth Karnaim (Genesis 14:5). But after Abraham defeated Kedorlaomer, the Rephaites rebuilt and became stronger.

Deuteronomy 3:13 says, "The whole region of Argob in Bashan used to be known as a land of the Rephaites." Cool! "Argob—the Land of Giants!" There were gobs of giants in Argob. Not only that but Bashan was chock-full of cities, and "all these cities were fortified with high walls and with gates and bars, and there were also a great many unwalled villages" (Deuteronomy 3:5). (Imagine a kid like you darting down a crowded street, trying to keep from getting stepped on by hundreds of giants!)

Then something happened. We don't know what—whether war or disease—but the powerful, prosperous giants of Bashan began dying out. Maybe they had become too lazy and fat? Giants probably already had heart trouble, so you just know that a fat giant's asking for trouble! Soon they were down to a remnant, and normal-sized Amorites took over.

Then there wasn't even a remnant left. By the time the Israelites showed up, "only Og king of Bashan was left of the remnant of the Rephaites" (Deuteronomy 3:11). More about Og later.

CLIMB TO NORTH CANAAN'S REPHAITES

Now slosh through the Jordan River and head south. Cross the Jezreel Valley and you're in the land of the mountain giants, the Rephaites of north Canaan! These towering, scowling, hairy

brutes were later called the Anakites of the hill country of Israel, but from the earliest days they were simply called Rephaites (Genesis 15:18–21; Joshua 11:21).

When Abraham came into Canaan, he traveled south on the road that wound along the tops of the central hills. Back then the hills were covered with thick forests of oak, pine, poplar, willow, bay, cypress, and fir. There were also groves of fig, olive, almond, and apricot trees. Shady country.

The first giants Abraham would've met on that road (if he met any) were these Rephaites. They lived in the forested hills as far north as Mount Gilboa. Hundreds of years later, when the Israelites invaded Canaan, the Rephaites were still there—and these mountains were still called the land of the Rephaites (Genesis 15:18–21; Joshua 17:15).

Fierce brown bears and ferocious lions also roamed these woods. The giants who lived there had to defend themselves from these beasts. Mind you, they wouldn't have worried too much. Even a lion would have to be mighty hungry to attack a ten-foot tall, 900-pound giant hefting a heavy ax.

Speaking of axes, some of the giants up in these forests probably earned their living as woodcutters. Paul Bunyan was just a tall tale, but the Canaanites did need lumber, so very likely there were giant lumberjacks! They would've been good at it.

Both times mountain giants are mentioned in the Bible, it says they lived near people called Perizzites (Genesis 15:18–21; Joshua 17:15). Perizzites means "Those Who Dwell in Unwalled Towns." The Perizzites and Rephaites probably felt so safe high up in their mountain forests that they didn't even need walled towns.

These fearsome forest fellows were some of the most rugged of all the giants, but even they would eventually meet their doom ... as you shall see.

Giants' Homes

Did giants live in caves? Maybe. The village of Beit Jibrin is in the western foothills of the Hebron Mountains. Jibrin comes from the Hebrew word *gibborim*, which means "mighty ones" or "giants," so the name Beit Jibrin means "House of the Giants."

Beside the village are 1,250 acres of caverns that make up one of the most amazing cave cities in the world. There are eight hundred caves there. Some of them measure up to four hundred feet long and have ceilings eighty feet high. One cave alone has sixty chambers.

These caverns have been hacked out of the rock with metal picks, so you know it wasn't gophers digging them. Local folklore says that giants once inhabited these caves. The Avvites did live a few miles to the west, and some scholars believe that some Avvites fled inland when the Philistines conquered them. So maybe some holed up in these caves.

THE BEACHFRONT AVVITES

Take a camel south and west and soon you come to the coast where the Mediterranean Sea pounds on the shore and seagulls circle. This was the land of the Avvites—the coastal giants. Apparently, the Avvites loved the smell of salt air. Or maybe they enjoyed playing in the sand. Who knows? Can't you just picture ten-foot titans stretched out on the beach?

Like the other giants of central Canaan, the Avvites were also called Anakites. The Bible says giants lived in the Philistine cities of Gaza, Gath, and Ashdod on the coast (Joshua 11:22). Of course, the Avvites were living there looooong before the Philistines arrived in their ships. The Avvites were stomping along the beaches way back in Abraham's day. Around that time, the Egyptians wrote nasty letters called execration texts and cursed Ashdod, calling it "the City of the Giants."

We don't know much about the Avvites except that they probably ate a lot of fish. And they didn't like Egyptians much. Whether they swam in the sea or not, we can't say.

About the time that Joshua and the Israelites invaded Canaan, the Philistines sailed from Caphtor (Crete) and landed on the Avvites' coast. And that was pretty much the end of the Avvites. "As for the Avvites who lived in villages as far as Gaza, the Caphtorites coming out from Caphtor destroyed them and settled in their place" (Deuteronomy 2:23).

You notice that it says the Avvites living in the villages got wiped out. The villages were unprotected. But some living in the walled cities of Ashdod, Gaza, and Gath survived. Hundreds of years later, Goliath and other giants still lived in Gath (Joshua 11:22; 1 Samuel 17:4; 2 Samuel 21:15–22).

Big Stuff

Imagine the daily life of giants like Og and Goliath—the lifestyles of the huge and heavy. Everything about them would have been supersized.

- Sandal sizes must have been enormous—like about a size fifty! Shaq O'Neal's basketball shoe would've looked like a kid's running shoe compared with Og's clogs.

- To make clothing for a giant would've taken about five times the amount of wool it took to dress a regular Canaanite. Can you imagine lending a giant your favorite T-shirt?

- The bowls from which a giant ate would've been as big as a basin or a large salad bowl.

- The beds had to be monstrous. King Og's bed "was made of iron and was more than thirteen feet long and six feet wide" (Deuteronomy 3:11). That's twice as long as your bed!

- To avoid bumping their heads on the rafters, giants must have had to live in houses with ceilings twelve to fourteen feet high. Ceilings today average eight feet high.

- Pets: To giants, normal dogs were as small as puppies. Now, a leopard! There'd have been a decent-sized kitty cat! Problem was, leopards really scratch up the furniture!

- Transportation: Giants had to walk everywhere. They were too large and heavy for donkeys or chariots. Camels can carry nine hundred pounds a short distance, but for longer trips they can only carry four hundred pounds. Too bad there were no elephants in Canaan!

- Farm tools for these guys would have been mammoth. An ax head would've weighed about thirty pounds.

- Meat: Giants needed large flocks of cattle, goats, and sheep to fill their monstrous stomachs. Fortunately, Hebron, the Anakites' capital, was a center for shepherds and herders. (Presumably, the giants ate the sheep rather than the shepherds!)

- Most farms in Canaan were six to eight acres in size. Giants would've needed forty to sixty acres of gigantic gardens, vast vineyards, and sprawling grain fields.

- Certain jobs were tough for giants, so they probably had normal-sized servants do those. For example, bending way, way down to harvest wheat and barley would've been back-breaking for a giant!

49

Ambling Anakites

The Anakites of Hebron were a famous giant clan, but they weren't there in Abraham's time. Abraham settled in the town of Mamre, and Mamre was right beside Hebron. A few hundred years later, Hebron was the capital city of the Anakites (Genesis 13:18; Joshua 14:15). But the Bible doesn't mention one giant living there in Abraham's day. Back then Hebron was a Hittite city.

The Anakites obviously migrated there later, and you can only imagine what they did to the Hittites. (Probably they hit them.) So where did these giants come from? Maybe some giants from the mountains of northern Canaan moved south. Or when the Ammonites conquered the Zamzummites, maybe some waded west across the Jordan River and settled near Hebron. We may never know.

GET STRONGER

The Bible says the giants were "numerous." So how many lived in Canaan in Abraham's day? Well, if there were 3,000,000 Canaanites back then, and the Rephaites were one of ten Canaanite nations (Genesis 15:18–21)—you'd divide 3,000,000 by 10 and get 300,000. That might be a good estimate of the number of people in each of the ten nations. But since giants need lots of space and food, let's cut that figure way down to 50,000 giants—or even 25,000. That's still a lot.

Here's the punch line: God promised pip-squeak Abraham that his descendants would inherit the giants' land—but how? There was a bunch of giants to deal with.

Abe ended up waiting years and years to have one kid! (Genesis 15:5, 18–21; 21:5). Today Abraham's kids number in the millions, and the giants are long gone. Abraham ended up the strongest with the mostest because he started out strong in faith (Romans 4:18–21). Remember that a big part of being strong is to start out strong in spirit.

HERE COME THE HEBREWS!

The Israelites started out small, but after 430 years in Egypt they increased to nearly 3,000,000—and 603,550 of those were fighting men (Numbers 1:45–46; Psalm 105:10–12). After leaving Egypt, the Israelites traveled through the desert for two years, then plunked down their tents at Kadesh Barnea, just south of Canaan. From there Moses sent twelve spy guys—including Joshua and Caleb—to check out the land.

Giant Veggies

If giants were alive today, guess which state they oughta move to? Alaska! Because of its looooooong days in the summer, Alaska's vegetables grow to humongous sizes. Look at how much these record-breaking Alaskan veggies weigh.

cabbage	105 $\frac{1}{2}$ lb.
zucchini	37 $\frac{1}{2}$ lb.
beet	42 $\frac{3}{4}$ lb.
carrot	19 lb.
celery	49 lb.
cauliflower	31 $\frac{1}{4}$ lb.
lettuce	18 lb.
kohlrabi	43 $\frac{3}{4}$ lb.
Swiss chard	71 $\frac{3}{4}$ lb.
broccoli	35 lb.

God had already told them Canaan was a good land, "a land with streams and pools of water ... with wheat and barley, vines and fig trees, pomegranates, olive oil and honey; a land where bread will not be scarce and you will lack nothing" (Deuteronomy 8:7–9). When the spies returned to camp forty days after they left, they admitted, yeah, it was a land of milk and honey and pomegranates, all right. But!

Then they got this scared look in their eyes and said, "The people who live there are powerful, and the cities are fortified and very large. We even saw descendants of Anak there" (Numbers 13:28). Verse 33 says, "The descendants of Anak come from the Nephilim." In other words, giants!

Caleb saw where this little conversation was headed, so he shouted, "We should go up and take possession of the land, for we can certainly do it" (Numbers 13:30).

The other ten spies argued, "We can't attack those people; they are stronger than we are... All the people we saw there are of great size... We seemed like grasshoppers in our own eyes, and we looked the same to them" (Numbers 13:31–33).

Caleb replied, "Grasshoppers, smashhoppers!" Just kidding. Actually Caleb said, "If the LORD is pleased with us, he will lead us into that land ... and will give it to us. Only do not rebel against the LORD. And do not be afraid of the people of the land, because we will swallow them up. Their protection is gone, but the LORD is with us" (Numbers 14:8–9).

The Israelites didn't believe Caleb. Why? They were afraid. They didn't have the faith to swallow giants. God punished the Israelites for their disbelief and sent them packing for forty years in the dusty desert till all the doubting older dudes had died. Only Caleb and Joshua survived to enter the land (Numbers 13; 14:1–10, 20–35).

Mountains of Food

Your body uses food to create energy, and the amount of energy that food creates is measured in calories. If you play computer games all day long, you don't need many calories. If you're active, you need lots. And if you're extremely active—like you're lifting weights or you're a professional soldier—you really need the calories. So let's compare normal people with giants.

	Age	Pounds	Height	Activity	Calories/day
Boys	8	55	4 ft. 2 in.	Normal	1,480
	12	85	4 ft. 10 in.	Normal	1,880
Adult men	40	150	5 ft. 8 in.	Normal	2,400
	40	150	5 ft. 8 in.	Active	3,200
Goliath	40	850	9 ft. 9 in.	Active	11,200
King Og	50	1,200+	11 ft. 0 in.	Normal	12,000

A normal-sized man who does muscle training needs about 3,200 calories a day. A giant like Goliath, who was constantly training for war, would've needed 11,200 calories a day!

A normal meal for a good-sized man has 600 to 800 calories. So Goliath would have needed nearly fourteen massive meals a day! Picture the biggest meal you've seen your dad put away at a family barbecue. Goliath would have cleaned off the entire picnic table before burping and then flopping down on the picnic blanket. And if you wonder where the watermelon went, well, you get three guesses.

Just to keep up his muscle mass, Goliath probably needed to eat something like a three-pound ostrich egg for breakfast, an entire ham roast for lunch, and a whole leg of lamb for dinner. And that's not counting veggies! French fries, nothing. Picture this guy popping entire potatoes!

And King Og, at eleven feet and 1,200 pounds? Don't even get me started. Can you imagine the look on the cook's face as Og ducks into an all-you-can-eat restaurant? He'd clean them out. Plates? Ha! He'd be eating out of the metal serving bins!

ANAK AND THE ANAKITES

What had the spies seen that scared them spitless and witless? They had seen cities full of Anakites—powerful, colossal human beings.

When Abraham lived at Hebron, there were no giants there. By Joshua's day, Hebron was the Anakites' capital. In Abraham's day, "Anak who?" In Joshua's day, Anakites were so famous that you measured other giants by how they compared with the Anakites.

The Anakites, of course, were Rephaites-type giants. They only made a name for themselves when a giant named Anak (meaning "long-necked") became ruler. Anak must've been just about the biggest, strongest, meanest giant who had ever lived. He apparently became head of all the Rephaite clans of Canaan (west of the Jordan River) and united them.

THE GIANTEST GIANT

But wait! As tough as Anak was, he had an even greater, stronger granddaddy giant by the name of Arba. Joshua 15:13 says, "Arba was the forefather of Anak." Now, the name Arba means "Strength of Baal," and this guy probably was a strong bruiser. Joshua 14:15 says, "Hebron used to be called Kiriath Arba [City of Arba] after Arba, who was the greatest man among the Anakites."

The city probably had been named after Arba because he built it up from the sleepy little sheep town it was in Abraham's day into a fortress with high walls (Numbers 13:22, 28).

When did Arba take over the city and build it up? Numbers 13:22 says, "Hebron had been built seven years before Zoan in Egypt." Now, Zoan had been built up by Pharaoh Seti eighty-four years before the Hebrews left Egypt. Do the math: Arba had turned Hebron into his city ninety-one years before the Hebrews showed up.

Kiriath Arba, or Hebron, was still a trading center for shepherds and herders, and it was on the main trade route from Canaan to Egypt. So the giants didn't lack for any luxuries. Caravans came through all the time. And grapes, pomegranates, and figs grew around the city.

Abraham and Isaac and Jacob were buried in a cave in Mamre, two miles north of Hebron (Genesis 49:29–31), and the giants controlled this too. The Hebrew spies sent by Moses may have stopped to look at this holy site, because they cut down grapes in the Valley of Eshcol right beside it (Numbers 13:23).

Three Giant Leaders

The Bible says the giants Ahiman, Sheshai, and Talmai, the descendants of Anak, lived in Hebron (Numbers 13:22, 28, 32). These three hulkin' bruisers are mentioned several times as the leaders of the Anakites, so let's have a closer look at them.

Ahiman's name means "Brother of a Portion," which in Hebrew works out to mean, "A Gift." (We don't know if Ahiman thought he was God's gift to the giants, but whoever named him thought he was special.)

Sheshai's name means "Free, Noble," which is pretty cool— although some scholars think it means "Whitish." (One thing we know for sure is that it doesn't mean "Sushi.")

Talmai's name means "Bold, Spirited," and if he lived up to his name, Talmai would've been courageous in battle—and loud. The name *Talmai* can also mean "Furrow, Ridge," but who would call a kid "Dirt Heap"?

These three humongous humans ruled from Hebron and lorded it over two other cities of giants, Anab and Debir (Joshua 11:21). Debir was near Hebron. Anab, whose name means "Hill," was south of Debir. Anakites also lived in mountain villages around Hebron (Joshua 10:36–37).

The Big Cities

The Hebrew spies were wowed by the fortress cities of Canaan. They said, "The cities are fortified and very large" (Numbers 13:28). They had "walls up to the sky" (Deuteronomy 9:1). Remember, the Hebrews were professional city builders back in Egypt (Exodus 1:11). They knew a big city when they saw one.

Cities in Canaan were often built atop hills for extra protection, and those in the plains sat on one-hundred-foot-tall city mounds—and then the city walls rose above that! Mizpah wasn't even a big city, but it had walls thirty-five feet high and fifteen to twenty feet thick. Jericho had walls eighteen feet thick. Larger cities had monumental walls. Shechem had a city gate measuring fifty-nine feet wide by sixty-five feet high!

Many cities had extra protection—a sloping rampart (outer wall). A rampart eighty feet wide and twenty feet high surrounded Shechem, and guard chambers and towers surrounded the city gate.

Unwalled farming villages surrounded the cities, and during times of war the villagers rushed into the cities for protection. To enjoy this protection, they had to pay money to their giant rulers.

THE VALLEY OF GIANTS

The Anakites also lived as far north as the Valley of Rephaites—the Valley of Giants—between Jerusalem and Bethlehem. This three-mile-long valley was important to the Anakites because it had huge fields for growing wheat (Joshua 18:16; Isaiah 17:5). Bethlehem overlooked the valley, and its name means "House of Bread." Go figure! Giants apparently liked bread as much as anyone, although their loaves must've been huge.

GET DEEPER

It's easy to understand why the Anakites had the spies shakin' in their sandals. They were fearsome giants. Moses told the Israelites, "The people are strong and tall—Anakites!" Then he said, "But be assured today that the LORD your God ... will destroy them; he will subdue them before you. And you will drive them out" (Deuteronomy 9:1–3).

Do you have problems that are greater and stronger than you? Maybe you need to get better grades in school, or to stand up for what is right. It could be just about anything that's too big for you to overcome alone. Put your faith in God to help you do what's right even if it's hard. Pray, hand over your concerns to God, and he'll give you the strength to conquer giants!

THE CONQUEST BEGINS

Okay, so the Israelites were scared of the giants of Hebron, so for forty years they wandered in the desert instead. But after the giant-fearing oldies had all died, the younger generation of Israelites was ready to march in and conquer. Only they didn't attack the Anakites from the south. They circled around the Dead Sea and came into the land of Heshbon, north of Moab.

They wanted to cross the Jordan River into Canaan, but Sihon king of Heshbon wouldn't let them walk through his land. He ordered his army to attack them. Big mistake! The Israelites stomped him.

Then the Israelites marched north toward the kingdom of Bashan. Now, this kingdom was also inhabited by normal-sized Amorites, but there was a difference. Bashan had a supersized king named Og! This guy was so humongous that he'd have won every pie-eating contest in Canaan—if they'd had pies back then.

OG, KING OF BASHAN

Deuteronomy 3:11 says, "Only Og king of Bashan was left of the remnant of the Rephaites. His bed was made of iron and was more than thirteen feet long and six feet wide." Giving him one foot of wiggle room on top and on the bottom means that Og was, oh, about eleven feet tall. He probably weighed at least 1,200 pounds.

Bashan used to be a kingdom of giants, but by Joshua's day the Rephaites had nearly all died out. Only Og remained, the last giant in a long line of titanic tyrants (Genesis 14:5; Joshua 12:4; 13:12). Og's name means "Giant."

Josephus tells us that Og was not bad-looking for a giant: "Og had very few equals, either in the largeness of his body or handsomeness of his appearance. He was also a man of great activity in the use of his hands." Maybe that "great activity" with his hands had to do with stuffing food in his mouth?

King Og had two capital cities, Ashtaroth and Edrei, and he ruled over sixty fortified cities with high walls and with gates and bars. He also reigned over oodles of unwalled villages (Deuteronomy 3:4–5). Whoa! That's a lot of land and one heap of cities! No wonder they needed a giant king!

The Amorites probably made Og king because Og was so—well, huge! He must have been impressive! We don't know how smart Og was or how well he reigned, but at least the Amorites could point up at him and boast, "There's our king!"

Og apparently had a wife, because he had several sons (Numbers 21:35). We don't know these boys' names, or even if they were giants like their whopper-sized papa, but when they died, there were no more giants in Bashan.

THE HARDER THEY FALL

Og's armies marched out to fight the Israelites, and they battled at the city of Edrei. Moses said, "The LORD our God also gave into our hands Og king of Bashan and all his army.

We struck them down, leaving no survivors. At that time we took all his cities. There was not one of the sixty cities that we did not take from them—the whole region of Argob, Og's kingdom" (Deuteronomy 3:3–4).

The Israelites carried off all the livestock and plunder from Og's cities. They entered Og's palace and probably snacked in his oversized kitchen! In fact, they even carried off his enormous bed! There's no telling what they wanted it for, and it looks like they passed it off to the Ammonites, because next thing we hear, Og's bed was on display in the city of Rabbah in Ammon (Deuteronomy 3:11).

How Giants Fought

Giants were huge and weighty and their weapons were deadly and heavy. They must have been terrifying fighting machines. You'd definitely wanna be somewhere else when one waded into combat swinging a thirty-pound battle-ax. We're talking bone-crushing force. Their weapons would've hacked clear through shields, body armor, bones—you name it.

Another thing: A normal warrior had arms two and a half feet long and a sword two feet long. That's a four-and-a-half-foot reach. A Rephaite, meanwhile, had arms three and a half feet long and a sword three feet long. That's a six-and-a-half-foot reach. They were killing regular soldiers before the little guys got close enough to do any damage.

Giants like Goliath and Ishbi-Benob (another giant of Gath) were also deadly with battle spears (1 Samuel 17:7; 2 Samuel 21:16). Warriors didn't throw spears. They thrust with them, using two hands. Normal-sized spears were about six feet long, but giants' spears would've been ten feet long!

Giants did throw javelins, which were kind of like skinny spears (1 Samuel 17:6). A normal guy could chuck a javelin 200 feet, though maybe not super-accurately. A giant with good aim might bring you down from 300 feet away.

Got all this? Good. Now you know why the Canaanites asked, "Who can stand up against the Anakites?" (Deuteronomy 9:2).

With the death of Og and sons, there were no more giants east of the Jordan River. The Emites were gone, the Zamzummites were gone, and now the Ogs were gone. But there were still thousands—maybe tens of thousands—of terrifying, smelly, snarling giants waiting for the Israelites in Canaan.

TRAVELING CONQUERORS

The Israelites' first battles in Canaan weren't against giants but against regular-sized Amorites and Canaanites. First Jericho fell, then Ai. When the Amorites in Gibeon made peace with Israel, Gibeon was attacked by five Amorite kings—the kings of Jerusalem, Jarmuth, Lachish, and Eglon, plus Hoham king of Hebron (Joshua 10:1–5). (That's Hoham, not Ho-hum!)

Did you catch that? The king of Hebron was there, too—and Hebron was the Anakites' capital city. So was Hoham a giant? The Bible doesn't say, but obviously the three giants Ahiman, Sheshai, and Talmai were no longer ruling Hebron. Forty years had passed. They were still living there but they were old. Hoham was now king.

Or he was till Joshua killed him and hung him up in a tree.

After the Israelites defeated the Amorites, they attacked Hebron. (This is the big battle! Finally!) They took the city

and wiped out its inhabitants and conquered the surrounding villages as well. They then marched seven miles southwest to Debir, stormed its gates, and took that city too (Joshua 10:36–39).

So was that the end of the giants? Was that the end of Ahiman, Sheshai, and Talmai? Nope. The war in Canaan lasted seven years, and this was, like, only the first year of the war.

The Israelites attacked the giants' cities, but many Anakites apparently fled into the mountains. The Israelites didn't move into the cities at this time. Instead they headed north to fight battles up there. So guess what? The giants sneaked back into Hebron and Debir, refortified the walls, and prepared for round two.

Canaanites & Giants

If the giants were so big and fierce—and they were—why didn't they overrun the land and wipe out normal-sized Canaanites? Well, the Anakites did take over most of the hills. They lived in "all the hill country of Judah, and … all the hill country of Israel" (Joshua 11:21).

The giants did run a few valleys, such as the Valley of Rephaites (Joshua 18:16), but mostly these oversized guys ruled the hills, and regular Canaanites ruled the valleys and plains. Wonder why?

Here's a clue: When the Hebrew tribe of Manasseh needed more land, they had two not-so-fun choices: (1) go up into the forested hills and drive out the giants, or (2) go down to the Jezreel Valley and drive out the Canaanites. The Manassites went after the giants. Why? Because the Canaanites down in the plain had iron chariots (Joshua 17:11–18).

It looks like the Canaanites' iron chariots had kept the giants back. No one, no matter how big, is gonna stand in front of rumbling chariots. Giants were big, sure, but were just too slow and clumsy to fight fast, zippy-zip chariot armies on the open plains.

Big Guys Running Scared

Remember Caleb? The spy who believed God would help the Israelites conquer the giants? After seven years, the wars of Canaan were coming to an end. Now it was time to go back and finish rooting out the giants. Caleb gathered the men of Judah and said to Joshua, "I was forty years old when Moses the servant of the LORD sent me from Kadesh Barnea to explore the land... Now then, just as the LORD promised, he has kept me alive for forty-five years... So here I am today, eighty-five years old! I am still as strong today as the day Moses sent me out; I'm just as vigorous to go out to battle now as I was then. Now give me this hill country that the LORD promised me that day. You yourself heard then that the Anakites were there and their cities were large and fortified, but, the LORD helping me, I will drive them out just as he said" (Joshua 14:7,10–12).

Wow! How do you answer a guy like that? Joshua did the only thing he could do—he blessed Caleb and gave him Hebron (Joshua 14:13–14).

Picture Caleb, eighty-five years old and still just itching to run up the mountain and battle giants! You gotta admire that! And did he succeed? Yup! The men of Judah helped him, and they attacked

Hebron and defeated Ahiman, Sheshai, and Talmai (Judges 1:10). More importantly, God helped Caleb!

So did those three giants fight? Did they die in battle? Nah. They ran away. "From Hebron Caleb drove out the three Anakites—Sheshai, Ahiman and Talmai" (Joshua 15:14). Those three giant geezers were so scared of Caleb that while his army was at the front gate, they slipped out a back door and took off a-running! We don't know where they went, but they weren't hanging around Hebron.

Remember the proverb "Who can stand up against the Anakites?" Ha ha ha! Sounds like a joke about now, doesn't it?

THE PRINCESS AND THE GIANT

Now here comes a tale of a courageous young warrior who killed giants to win the hand of a beautiful princess. You'd think this was straight out of a fairy tale, but you would be wrong. It actually happened.

You see, after Caleb defeated the giants at Hebron, he decided to settle down there. So now who would lead the army against Debir? Not too many other Israelites were eager to fight giants—not even to get their plunder.

But would someone do it for love? Caleb thought so. He was one of the top leaders of Israel (Numbers 13:1–6). He had a beautiful daughter named Acsah. Acsah's name means "Ankle Bangle" (that's a thin gold bracelet around a woman's ankle).

So Caleb said—and this is what it sounded like in Hebrew— "I will give my daughter Ankle Bangle in marriage to the man who attacks and captures the City of Books" (Joshua 15:16).

There was this young warrior named Othniel. His name means "God Is Force," and he certainly believed that. Othniel was so smitten with love for Ankle Bangle, er,

Acsah, that he led an army against Debir and took it. We don't know the details of this battle and how well the giants

fought, whether they made their last stand in the library, or how many Israelites they killed before they went down, but down they went.

After that there was a big wedding. It would be great if we could tell you that Othniel and Acsah settled down on a farm, had lots of kids, and grew old in peace—but alas, it was not meant to be. When Othniel was about fifty, foreign invaders conquered Israel and ruled it for eight years. Then Othniel again rose up, led an army, and drove out their oppressors (Judges 3:7–11). Powerful stuff! But who's surprised? Here's a guy who started his career by killing giants!

HUNTING DOWN STRAY GIANTS

Joshua had led the armies of Israel for years, but now the wars were over. Caleb had reconquered Hebron, and Othniel had taken Debir. There was one last city of giants left to grab: Anab. So they nabbed Anab.

They also hunted down all the stray giants hiding out in the hills of Judah. That's probably when they finally tracked down Ahiman, Sheshai, and Talmai and finished them off. "At that time Joshua went and destroyed the Anakites from the hill country: from Hebron, Debir and Anab, from all the hill country of Judah, and from all the hill country of Israel. Joshua totally destroyed them and their towns. No Anakites were left in Israelite territory" (Joshua 11:21–22).

Giant Libraries

In Joshua's day, about 600 years after Abraham, the giant Anakites had a city in south Canaan called Debir (Joshua 11:21). The giants called it Kiriath Sepher, which means "City of Scribes" or "City of Books." The city's other name was Kiriath Sannah, which means "City of Instruction" (Joshua 15:49). Bible scholars believe Kiriath Sepher was a major center of learning and culture for all of Canaan. It probably had a huge library full of scrolls, and was the city where giants went to learn.

Can't you just picture a dozen heavy, hairy giants sitting around mumbling loudly as they read? You can be sure they weren't sitting in ordinary-sized desks!

What were their books about? No idea. All the monster scrolls seem to have been torched when the Israelites conquered the city (Judges 1:11–13).

GET SMARTER

British fairy tales say most giants were dim-witted. But that's not true. Sure, they were slow and maybe a little lazy because they were so heavy. But being slow physically doesn't mean they were slow mentally. In fact, since the Anakites had an entire city devoted to books and learning, many giants obviously loved to read and study.

You know, if the giants, bad as they were, loved to learn, how much more should you read and study? Your advantage is that if you love God and apply yourself, God will help you learn. Remember Daniel and his pals? "To these four young men God gave knowledge and understanding of all kinds of literature and learning" (Daniel 1:17).

CONQUERING MOUNTAIN GIANTS

Now Joshua gathered the twelve tribes of Israel and divided the land of Canaan among them. There was one teensy problem. A lot of the land he gave to the tribes hadn't been conquered yet. Each tribe was responsible for conquering the Canaanites who still lived in its backyard.

One day the leaders of Ephraim and Manasseh came to Joshua complaining that he hadn't given them enough land. They said, "Why have you given us only ... one portion for an inheritance? We are a numerous people" (Joshua 17:14).

"If you are so numerous," Joshua answered, "and if the hill country of Ephraim is too small for you, go up into the forest and clear land for yourselves there in the land of the Perizzites and Rephaites" (Joshua 17:15).

Rephaites? Whoa! These were the mountain giants! How would you like to have gone hunting giants in the mountain forests? Not only did these enormous brutes know their mountains really well, but they were armed with huge axes and spears. And they were hiding behind oak trees. Just waiting. And breathing heavily.

But the Israelites did it. We don't know the details of those battles, because they hadn't invented the evening news yet and there were no reporters on the front lines. But finally the mountain giants were gone. The Israelites had destroyed them all.

GET COOLER

Okay, so Othniel risked his life for a beautiful princess when no one else had the guts to. Why did he do it? He wanted to marry Acsah. So what's the lesson here for you? Do you need to bungee jump off the Brooklyn Bridge to impress some cute girl? No. But it does mean there will be times when you will need to put out extra effort—maybe a lot of extra effort—to help those you care for, such as family and friends. Maybe you'll have to get down, dirty, and sweaty cleaning your grandparents' garage. As Paul said, "Christ's love compels us" (2 Corinthians 5:14).

Okay, for those of you who insist that a book about giants isn't complete without talking about Goliath, let's shine the spotlight on that colossal guy from Gath (1 Samuel 17). Goliath looms large in the pages of the Bible, but as you know by now, he wasn't the only giant who ever lived. Not by a long shot!

Goliath belonged to the Avvite clan. The Philistines had ruled their lands for hundreds of years, so by now the Avvites pretty much considered themselves Philistines—except of course that they were much, much bigger.

We've already mentioned Goliath's vital stats. First Samuel 17:4 says, "He was over nine feet tall," but the original Hebrew is more exact. It says his height was "six cubits and a span." A cubit is 18 inches (6 x 18 = 108 inches = 9 feet) plus a span, which was 9 inches. If you do the math, you'll find out that Goliath was nine feet nine inches tall.

Weight Lifting

Just exactly how strong were giants? Amos 2:9 says they were "strong as the oaks." That's strong as the oaks, not strong as an ox. An ox was what a giant lifted over his head. Seriously.

A modern-day Olympic weight lifter weighing only 115 pounds has lifted over 500 pounds, and a 250-pound Australian has lifted over 900 pounds, so how much could an 850- or 1,200-pound giant have lifted? Archaeologists haven't ever found ancient giant barbells, but a good guess is that Goliath could easily have put a 1,000-pound ox over his head. Easily. How far he could have thrown that ox is the question.

Giants' Gods

We know that giants worshiped gods just like regular Canaanites did, because Goliath "cursed David by his gods" (1 Samuel 17:43). A pretty bad thing to do, but it does show that Goliath was religious in a sick kind of way.

Some giants' names show the gods they worshiped. The name of one giant, Arba, can mean "Strength of Baal." In fact, the giants of Syria, to the north, were known as the Rephaites of Baal.

It would be great if we could say that there were bad giants and then there were good giants. Only problem is, not one Bible giant was a friend of God's people. Every giant we know about was bad.

When you do the math on that, it works out to Goliath weighing about 850 pounds. And he was in top fighting shape, 'cause he had been a fighter since he was young (1 Samuel 17:33). Goliath was probably battling men at the age of twelve. Well, yeah! He would've been about seven and a half feet tall by then and would've weighed nearly 300 pounds! The day the Philistines faced the armies of Israel in the Valley of Elah, Goliath was at the height of his fighting ability.

Gath-guy was terrifying as he stomped out. He had a bronze helmet on his head and wore a coat of bronze scale armor weighing 125 pounds. Bronze armor protected his legs and he had a bronze javelin strapped on his back. His spear's shaft was megathick; its iron point weighed fifteen pounds. A little Philistine walked in front of Goliath carrying his shield (to protect Goliath's knees, I suppose).

With a voice like a built-in PA system, Goliath's challenge sounded basically like this to the Israelites, "Choose a champion to fight me! If he kills me, we'll be your slaves! If I kill him, you'll be our slaves."

When they heard Goliath, Saul and all the Israelites were terrified. No one wanted to fight this monster! Even Saul, who was bigger than most guys, decided he'd pass on this one.

GET STRONGER

Giants were naturally strong. They were just born that way. But some giants, like Goliath, were professional soldiers (1 Samuel 17:33) and were really, really strong. Goliath was so proud of his strength that he just "knew" no Israelite could fight him. In the end, however, a godly guy with a piece of gravel grounded him. Being strong is cool, but Jeremiah 9:23–24 warns, "Let not ... the strong man boast of his strength ..., but let him who boasts boast about this: that he understands and knows me, that I am the LORD." David knew God, Goliath didn't. Result? David won. There's nothing wrong with being strong. There's only a problem if you trust your muscles more than God (Jeremiah 17:5).

THE SCOOP ON DAVID

While Goliath's tonsils were still rattling, along comes David, leading a donkey loaded down with bread and cheese. You may have seen pictures of David as a nine-year-old kid—or even six years old—but you can definitely forget that. When he met Goliath, David was "a brave man and a warrior" (1 Samuel 16:18). He was at least eighteen. At that age he was probably a bit over five and a half feet tall and most likely weighed less than 150 pounds.

Super Strong

Robert Wadlow (the tallest man in modern history) was nearly nine feet tall and weighed almost 500 pounds, but that dude was skinny! Well, giants in the Bible weren't just tall. They were built sturdier and stronger, with thicker bones and bigger muscles.

Think about it: Goliath probably tipped the scales at 850 pounds, and according to the Bible (1 Samuel 17:4–7), he was weighed down with about 200 pounds of armor and weapons! Altogether he was a 1,050-pound human tank clanking around. You gotta believe Goliath was muscle-bound! And you just know he had to have huge, ox-sized bones to support all that weight and move.

Guess what? God even created Neanderthals, cave people with huge, thick bones and massive muscles. Their handgrip was twice as powerful as that of people today. (You wouldn't want to arm wrestle a Neanderthal.) So can you imagine how strong giants were?

What did David have going for him? Well, he was an excellent shot with a sling, that's for sure. And he had incredible guts! He had single-handedly killed a lion and a bear (1 Samuel 17:34–35). Still, the odds were way-over-the-top stacked against our guy.

DAVID ROCKS OUT

David was vastly outgunned, but he had one advantage: He trusted that God could do miracles. And God had made a specific promise about giants—that though they were strong and tall, God would destroy them (Deuteronomy 9:2–3).

When David closed in on Goliath, the giant cursed and mocked him. But David shouted, "You come against me with sword and spear and javelin, but I come against you in the

name of the LORD Almighty, the God of the armies of Israel"
(1 Samuel 17:45). He then informed Goliath that, oh yeah,
he was going to cut off his head.

This ticked Goliath off big time. He stomped closer. You
notice he didn't run. Remember, giants are not into this running business. But David dashed across the valley to meet
Goliath. With his feet flying through the grass, Dave reached
into his bag, took out a big ol' stone, and slung it! Kraaack!
The rock slammed into Goliath's forehead. It didn't bounce
off, either. The stone sank into his forehead.

High Elevation

According to scientists, people simply can't grow twice as tall as they are now. If a six-foot man weighing 200 pounds grew twice as tall, he would weigh a whopping 1,600 pounds—eight times as much! His weight would be more than human leg bones could support. That may be the reason why Bible giants never grew over ten to eleven feet tall, and even that high was tough.

There's an expression: "The bigger they are, the harder they fall." No kidding! If a man were twelve feet tall and he stumbled and fell, he'd hit the ground with sixteen times as much force as would a normal man. He wouldn't quite create his own crater—but bruises? You bet-cha. Broken bones? Likely.

Og was eleven feet tall and weighed 1,200 pounds. He would've crushed your bathroom scale! If you took him on the water slides, he'd get stuck inside the Tunnel of Doom!

You don't have to be a giant to weigh a lot. An American named Jon Brower Minnoch (1941–1983) was only six foot one inch tall but weighed 1,400 pounds! Jon claimed he wasn't handicapped a bit when he was 975 pounds, but by the time Jon weighed 1,400 pounds, he could hardly move. He was mostly fat and only a little bit muscle. It took thirteen people to roll him over in bed.

If Goliath could've said anything, he'd probably have said, "I am, like, totally stunned." But he didn't say a word. There was just a terrific ker-whummmpp! and all nine feet nine inches of giant tumbled face-first into the clover.

David ran and stood over him. Goliath's shield bearer had apparently split, 'cause no one was around to stop David from pulling Goliath's sword out of its scabbard. One good thrust and Mr. Giant was dead. Then David sliced off his head and held it up for everyone to get a good look at. (Yeah, uh, thanks, David. You can put it back now.) When the Philistines saw Goliath's head, they turned and ran.

COLLECTIBLE GIANT STUFF

There's just something about having giant trophies. Memorabilia means "collectible stuff," and giant memorabilia is even hotter than, say, baseball cards. Remember how the Ammonites kept King Og's thirteen-by-six-foot bed on display in Ammon?

According to Josephus, the Israelites even used to keep giants' bones on display. Josephus said, "The bones of these men are still [shown] to this very day."

No surprise then that after his battle with Goliath, David snagged a few trophies. "David took the Philistine's head and brought it to Jerusalem, and he put the Philistine's weapons in his own tent" (1 Samuel 17:54).

We don't know what the folks in Jerusalem did with Goliath's head (like, we should want to know?), and we don't know what happened to Goliath's spear and shield and javelin. But we do know that a few years later, Goliath's sword was with the high priest in Nob, where David picked it up again (1 Samuel 21:1, 8–9).

GET SMARTER

The big lesson about David fighting Goliath has always been that David trusted God and God helped him win. But let's also look at the smarter side of things, 'cause David definitely fought smarter, not harder. There was a method to his madness when he refused to wear King Saul's armor (1 Samuel 17:38–40). He would've been so weighed down that he couldn't have moved quickly. But why didn't he take Saul's sword? Hey, David didn't plan on even getting close. He knew that Goliath would cut him in two with his sword or impale him with his spear. So David did the smart thing. He brought Goliath down with a well-aimed sling-stone while he was still a distance away. Sometimes even giant problems have simple solutions if you use new ways to solve them.

THE LAST OF THE GIANTS

Some people ask, "If David brought Goliath down with one stone, why did he take five stones with him?" Well, there were still a few giants left, and maybe David wanted to be ready in case some of them stomped out, too.

These remaining biggies may have been Goliath's sons. The Bible calls them "sons of Rapha," and since the name Rapha means "The Giant," it could refer to Goliath. Or maybe "sons of Rapha" means they descended from their ancient ancestor, Rapha.

Big Boys

History is full of reports of giants, but most of these turned out to be exaggerations. Every once in a while there was some really tall guy, so word got around that he was a "giant," when actually he was just big. Okay, so how big does a guy have to be to be a giant?

The Israelites were slightly smaller than people today. Only the biggest Israelites reached six feet tall. For someone like Saul to be a head taller than any other Israelite (1 Samuel 9:2), he probably only had to be like six feet and a few inches. That's big, but it's still kind of shrimpy compared with real, honest-to-goodness giants.

Sure, there were a few oversized guys. When David was king, an Israelite named Benaiah "struck down a huge Egyptian" (2 Samuel 23:20–21), but even this Egyptian was no giant. Benaiah snatched the spear from the guy's hands and killed him with his own weapon. Pretty cool. But you just know he couldn't have done the old gimme-that-stick trick if the Egyptian had been ten feet tall and weighed 800 pounds!

Whoever their dad was, these big brutes didn't fight David that day. Instead they waited many years until David was old. One giant in particular waited a long time to kill David. Was he out to avenge Goliath's death? Let's check it out.

GOLIATH'S DEATH IS AVENGED

The Bible says, "There was a battle between the Philistines and Israel. David went down with his men to fight against the Philistines, and he became exhausted. And Ishbi-Benob, one of the descendants of Rapha, whose bronze spearhead weighed [seven and a half pounds] and who was armed with a new sword, said he would kill David" (2 Samuel 21:15–16).

Well now, Ishbi-Benob had vowed to kill David. He was a monster on a mission. Maybe Goliath was his dad and Benob wanted revenge. Or maybe he figured that if he killed the Israelites' king, they'd all scatter.

You notice Benob had "a new sword"—meaning it had never been used. Its iron blade was still razor sharp. The giant hadn't been fighting. So, like, what was he doing? Apparently, he was sitting out the battle, waiting on the sidelines until everyone was pooped out.

David was old by this time, probably nearly sixty, and on top of it he'd been fighting till he was exhausted. He was in no shape to fight any more Philistines, let alone a giant! So that's when Benob made his move. He plowed through the crowd, straight toward David.

We don't know if he got any blows in, but his huge sword would have nearly hacked David's shield in half. Fortunately, David's cousin Abishai was Mr. Johnny-on-the-spot and he struck the Philistine down and killed him (2 Samuel 21:17).

After that little fun time—not!—David's men told him, "No way are we letting you go out to battle again. You let us do the fighting!" Smart move, 'cause there were still some more giants out there.

GETTING TO GOB AND GEZER

That battle was over, but the Philistines were still playing the giant card. "In the course of time, there was another battle with the Philistines, at Gob. At that time Sibbecai the Hushathite killed Saph, one of the descendants of Rapha" (2 Samuel 21:18). The Bible doesn't tell us the details of this battle, but 1 Chronicles 20:4 says it took place at the town of Gezer. (That's not geezer like some old guy. That's Gezer and it means "Cliff.")

Everyone was battling at the bottom of the cliff, in a place called Gob. Now, the name Gob means "Pit" or "Hollow." Scary stuff! Can you imagine fighting down in some hollow and suddenly this giant comes rushing down into it, swinging his sword? The Israelites didn't have much room to get out of his way. One guy didn't try to get away. His name was Sibbecai, and next thing you know, Saph is dead.

Cushites & Dinkas

South of Egypt live some very tall people. Isaiah 18:1–2 says that the people of Cush were "a people tall and smooth-skinned ... a people feared far and wide."

And even farther south along the Nile in the Sudd Swamp live the Dinkas. Lots of Dinkas are over seven feet tall. Manute Bol, a modern-day basketball player, comes from there, and this dude is seven feet seven inches tall. There's no surprise that he played for half a dozen different NBA teams.

The Dinkas are big, you gotta give them that. Okay, they are really big. In fact, they happen to be the tallest people on earth. But even they are not giants.

Saph is a name with lots of meanings. It means "Cup," "Bowl," "Basin," "Doorpost," "Gate," etc. Maybe Saph got tired of people calling him all that, because he also was known as Sippai, which means "Like a Basin." (Okay, not much of an improvement.)

And Sibbecai the Hushathite? Who was he? He was one of David's most awesome warriors, one of his top mighty men. Sibbecai also happened to be a captain of over 24,000 soldiers (1 Chronicles 11:26, 29; 27:11). His name means "God Is Intervening." Right!

A GIANT? OR JUST FULL OF BREAD?

Second Samuel 21:19 says, "In another battle with the Philistines at Gob, Elhanan son of Jaare-Oregim the Bethlehemite killed Goliath the Gittite, who had a spear with a shaft like a weaver's rod." Got that? Then 1 Chronicles 20:5 says, "Elhanan son of Jair killed Lahmi the brother of Goliath the Gittite, who had a spear with a shaft like a weaver's rod."

First we see amazing Elhanan slaying a giant called Goliath the Gittite. (This is not the Goliath who fought David about thirty years earlier. This was Goliath Junior. Apparently, Goliath was a popular name among giants.)

Second, we see Elhanan killing Lahmi the brother of Goliath the Gittite. (By the way, Lahmi's name means "Full of Bread." You really gotta wonder what some of these giant parents were thinking when they named their babies.)

Elhanan seems to hold the record for killing two giants in one battle. How on earth did he do it—especially since both giants had arrived that day with huge killer spears? Remember, warriors didn't throw spears; they held them in both hands and jabbed with them. And Goliath Junior and Lahmi fought at close range in the hollow of Gob, where they had all the advantage.

Just the same, Elhanan got them. So who was Elhanan? We don't know. He wasn't one of David's mighty men. He wasn't a captain over thousands. He wasn't really anyone—well, not before this happened. He was just another one of those tough kids from Bethlehem. His name means "God Is Gracious."

THE MULTIDIGIT MONSTER

"In ... another battle, which took place at Gath, there was a huge man with six fingers on each hand and six toes on each foot—twenty-four in all. He also was descended from Rapha. When he taunted Israel, Jonathan son of Shimeah, David's brother, killed him" (2 Samuel 21:20–21). Since we aren't given this giant's name, let's call him Old Twenty-Four.

The battle between Old Twenty-Four and a guy named Jonathan took place at Gath, Goliath's hometown. And wouldn't you know it, this giant was as proud and boastful as Goliath. He taunted Israel, and a taunt is something mocking, sarcastic, hurtful, and scornful.

Old Twenty-Four was talking trash because he was proud of his size and strength. He was sure he could clobber anyone. But the more he mocked, the madder the Israelites became.

Finally a gutsy guy named Jonathan, King David's own nephew, had heard enough. He moved in and mowed down this motormouth monster.

Giant-killing ran in David's family. First David killed Goliath. Then his cousin Abishai killed Ishbi-Benob. And finally Jonathan killed the multidigit monster.

Old Twenty-Four seems to have been the very last of the giants of Canaan. After he died in about 1000 B.C., the Rephaites are never mentioned again. The day he dropped in the dirt with a thud and the dust settled down, that was the end of the giants.

WHERE DID THE GIANTS GO?

When Jonathan killed Old Twenty-Four, that was the end of giants in Israel. But was it the end of all giants on earth? Maybe. Maybe not. There was one extra clan of giants, but they didn't live in Canaan, so they're not mentioned in the Bible. They were called the Rephaites of Baal, and they lived far up the coast, in what is now Syria.

In 1928, archaeologists dug up a big old dirt mound called Ras Shamra and uncovered the ancient Canaanite city of Ugarit. They found clay tablets that dated back to the days of Joshua, and some of these tablets talked a lot about the Rephaites, calling them the Rephaites of Baal. These Rephaites were 225 miles north of Canaan when the Israelites wiped out all the giants there. So what happened to them? Did they die out like the other giants? Or did they survive and migrate to new lands? Did some of them make it as far as Britain and Wales? Or were the Welsh and people from other nations simply remembering stories about the giants of Canaan and making up tales about their own giants? We simply don't know.

GET STRONGER

How did these warriors outfight giants? They didn't sling rocks from a distance. They were up close and personal! Well, Abishai may have been a lightweight compared with Ishbi-Benob, but he was still a lethal fighting machine. Here was a guy who attacked three hundred soldiers with his spear and killed them all (2 Samuel 23:18)! Sure, a lot of that was natural strength and ability, but a lot of it was also the fact that he was totally dedicated to his cause and trained to become a stronger, better fighter. He was disciplined, he was in shape, and he believed God was with him. Result? He could take out giants.

Don't neglect regular physical exercise, "for physical training is of some value" (1 Timothy 4:8). In fact, take a break from reading. Get down on the floor right now and do twenty push-ups!

CONCLUSION

Did you ever imagine that the Bible had so much cool information about giants? Hey, there's a lot more incredibly interesting stuff in the Bible, "new treasures as well as old" (Matthew 13:52). Read it and you'll see!

Giants were the ancient enemies of the Israelites. Many of the greatest heroes such as David, Joshua, Caleb, Othniel, Abishai, and others battled giants. It took tremendous courage, strength, and faith in God for these warriors to wrestle with the Rephaites. But they did it!

Several giant-killers came from Bethlehem: David, Abishai, Jonathan, and Elhanan. A thousand years later, another astonishing person was born in Bethlehem—Jesus Christ, God's Son. Jesus didn't battle ten-foot-tall giants, but he fought and defeated the most powerful dark power in the world, the Devil. By his death on the cross, Jesus destroyed the Devil's power and set us free to become God's children (Hebrews 2:14–15).

PRONUNCIATION KEY

Acsah — Ak'-sah

Ahiman — Ah-hi'-man

Ammon — Am'-mon

Amorites — Am'-o-rites

Anab — Ah'-nab

Anak — Ah'-nak

Anakites — An'-ak-ites

Arba — Ar'-bah

Ashdod — Ash'-dod

Avvites – Ay'-vites

Baal — Bay'-al

Bethlehem — Beth'-leh-hem

Caleb — Kay'-leb

Canaan — Kay'-nan

Debir — Day'-bur

Eglon — Egg'-lon

Elhanan — El-ha'-nan

Emites — Ee'-mites

Gath —Gath

Gaza — Gah'-zah

Hebron — Hee'-bron

Heshbon — Hesh'-bon

Hittite — Hit'-ite

Hoham — Ho'-ham

Ishbi-Benob — Ish'-bee Be'-nob

Israelites — Iz'-ray-el-ites

Jarmuth — Jar'-muth

Jerusalem — Jeh-ru'-sa-lem

Jezreel Valley — Jez'-reel Vall'-ee

Jonathan — Jon'-a-than

Joshua — Josh'-yu-uh

Judah — Ju'-duh

Kadesh Barnea — Ka'-desh Bar'-nee-uh

Kedorlaomer — Ked'-or-la-o'-mer

Kiriath Sepher/Sannah — Kir'-ee-ath Seh'-fur / Sah'-nah

Lachish — Lay'-kish

Lahmi — Lah'-mee

Mamre — Mam'-re

Manasseh/Manassites — Mah-nas'-seh / Mah-nas'-sites

Nephilim — Nef'-ill-im

Othniel — Oth'-nee-el

Philistines — Fi-lis'-teens

Ras Shamra — Ras Sham'-rah

Rephaites — Ref'-ah-ites

Saph — Saf

Sheshai — She'-shy

Sibeccai the Hushathite — Sib'-bek-eye the Hoo'-sha-thite

Syria — Seer'-ee-uh

Talmai — Tall-my

Ugarit — Yoo'-ga-rit

Zamzummites — Zam-zum'-ites

What is  SOUL GEAR ?

Based on Luke 2:52:
"And Jesus grew in wisdom and stature,
]and in favor with God and men (NIV)."

2:52 is designed just for boys 8-12!
This verse is one of the only verses in
the Bible that provides a glimpse of Jesus
as a young boy. Who doesn't wonder what
Jesus was like as a kid?

Become smarter, stronger, deeper,
and cooler as you develop
into a young man of God
with 2:52 Soul Gear™!

Zonderkidz

2:52 Soul Gear™ Nonfiction Books–

More ACTION & ADVENTURE–
straight from the pages of the Bible!

Bible Heroes & Bad Guys

Written by Rick Osborne, Marnie Wooding & Ed Strauss
Softcover 0-310-70322

Bible Wars & Weapons

Written by Rick Osborne, Marnie Wooding & Ed Strauss
Softcover 0-310-70323-9

Bible Fortresses, Temples & Tombs

Written by Rick Osborne
Softcover 0-310-70483-9

Weird & Gross Bible Stuff

Written by Rick Osborne
Softcover 0-310-70484-7

Amazing & Unexplainable Things in the Bible

Written by Rick Osborne & Ed Strauss
Softcover 0-310-70653-X

Creepy Creatures & Bizarre Beasts from the Bible

Written by Rick Osborne & Ed Strauss
Softcover 0-310-70654-8

The Ultimate Battle & Bible Prophecy

Written by Rick Osborne & Ed Strauss
Softcover 0-310-70776-5

Bible Angels & Deomons

Written by Rick Osborne & Ed Strauss
Softcover 0-310-70775-7

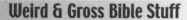
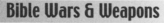

Available now at your local bookstore!

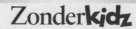

2:52 Soul Gear™ Laptop fiction books–

Technological thrillers that will keep you on the edge of your seat...

Laptop 1: Reality Shift

Written by Christopher P. N. Maselli
Softcover 0-310-70338-7

Laptop 2: Double-Take

Written by Christopher P. N. Maselli
Softcover 0-310-70339-5

Laptop 3: Explosive Secrets

Written by Christopher P. N. Maselli
Softcover 0-310-70340-9

Laptop 4: Power Play

Written by Christopher P. N. Maselli
Softcover 0-310-70664-5

Laptop 5: Dangerous Encounters

Written by Christopher P. N. Maselli
Softcover 0-310-70341-7

Laptop 6: Hot Pursuit

Written by Christopher P. N. Maselli
Softcover 0-310-70665-3

Laptop 7: Choke Hold

Written by Christopher P. N. Maselli
Softcover 0-310-70666-1

Laptop 8: Shut Down!

Written by Christopher P. N. Maselli
Softcover 0-310-70667-X

Check out other nonfiction books available in the 2:52 Soul Gear™ collection!

Lintball Leo's Not-So-Stupid Questions About Your Body

Written by Dr. Walt Larimore with John Riddle
Softcover 0-310-70545-2

The Book of Cool

Written by Tim Wesemann
Softcover 0-310-70696-3

GodQuest – Dare to Live the Adventure

Written by Rick Osborne
Softcover 0-310-70868-0

Reboot Your Brain
Byte-Sized Devotions for Boys

Written by Tim Shoemaker
Softcover 0-310-70719-6

Available now at your local bookstore!

Zonderkidz

Coming February 2005

Three friends, Dan, Peter, and Shelby, seek to discover the hidden mystery of Eckert House in this four-book series filled with adventure, mystery, and intrigue.

2:52 Mysteries of Eckert House: Hidden in Plain Sight (Book 1)

Written by Chris Auer
Softcover 0-310-70870-2

2:52 Mysteries of Eckert House: A Stranger, a Thief & a Pack of Lies (Book 2)

Written by Chris Auer
Softcover 0-310-70871-0

2:52 Mysteries of Eckert House: The Chinese Puzzle Box (Book 3)

Written by Chris Auer
Softcover 0-310-70872-9

2:52 Mysteries of Eckert House: The Forgotten Room (Book 4)

Written by Chris Auer
Softcover 0-310-70873-7

We want to hear from you. Please send your comments
about this book to us in care of the address below.
Thank you.

Zonder**kidz**.

5300 Patterson Avenue SE
Grand Rapids, MI 49530
www.zonderkidz.com